MORE!

Junior High Game Nights

MORE Wild & Crazy outreach events for junior high ministry

ZONDERVAN/YOUTH SPECIALTIES BOOKS

Professional Resources
Called to Care
Developing Student Leaders
Feeding Your Forgotten Soul
Growing Up in America
High School Ministry
How to Recruit and Train Volunteer
    Youth Workers (Previously released
    as Unsung Heroes)
Junior High Ministry
The Ministry of Nurture
Organizing Your Youth Ministry
The Youth Minister's Survival Guide
Youth Ministry Nuts and Bolts

Discussion Starter Resources
Amazing Tension Getters
Get 'Em Talking
High School TalkSheets
Hot Talks
Junior High TalkSheets
Option Plays
Tension Getters
Tension Getters Two

Special Needs and Issues
The Complete Student Missions
    Handbook
Divorce Recovery for Teenagers
Ideas for Social Action
Intensive Care: Helping Teenagers in
    Crisis
Rock Talk
Teaching the Truth About Sex
Up Close and Personal: How to Build
    Community in Your Youth Group

Youth Ministry Programming
Adventure Games
Creative Programming Ideas for Junior
    High Ministry
Creative Socials and Special Events
Good Clean Fun
Good Clean Fun, Volume 2
Great Games for City Kids
Great Ideas for Small Youth Groups
Greatest Skits on Earth
Greatest Skits on Earth, Volume 2

Holiday Ideas for Youth Groups (Revised
    Edition)
Junior High Game Nights
More Junior High Game Nights
On-Site: 40 On-Location Youth
    Programs
Play It! Great Games for Groups
Super Sketches for Youth Ministry
Teaching the Bible Creatively
The Youth Specialties Handbook for
    Great Camps and Retreats

4th-6th Grade Ministry
Attention Grabbers for 4th-6th Graders
Great Games for 4th-6th Graders
How to Survive Middle School
Incredible Stories
More Attention Grabbers for 4th-6th
    Graders
More Great Games for 4th-6th Graders
More Quick and Easy Activities for 4th-
    6th Graders
Quick and Easy Activities for 4th-6th
    Graders

Clip Art
ArtSource™ Volume 1—Fantastic
    Activities
ArtSource™ Volume 2—Borders,
    Symbols, Holidays, and Attention
    Getters
ArtSource™ Volume 3—Sports
ArtSource™ Volume 4—Phrases and
    Verses
ArtSource™ Volume 5—Amazing
    Oddities and Appalling Images
ArtSource™ Volume 6—Spiritual
    Topics
Youth Specialties Clip Art Book
Youth Specialties Clip Art Book,
    Volume 2

OTHER BOOKS BY DAN McCOLLAM AND KEITH BETTS

Junior High Game Nights
(Zondervan/Youth Specialties)

MORE! Junior High, Game Nights

MORE Wild & Crazy outreach events for junior high ministry

Dan McCollam & Keith Betts

Youth Specialties

Zondervan Publishing House
A Division of HarperCollinsPublishers

DISCLAIMER

Like life, this book contains games that, in an unfortunate combination of circumstances, could result in emotional or physical harm. Before you use a game, you'll need to evaluate it on its own merits for your group, for its potential risk, for necessary safety precautions and advance preparation, and for possible results. Youth Specialties, Inc., Zondervan Publishing House, and Dan McCollam and Keith Betts are not responsible for, nor have they any control over, the use or misuse of any games published in this book.

More Junior High Game Nights

Copyright © 1992 by Youth Specialties, Inc.

Youth Specialties Books, 1224 Greenfield Drive, El Cajon, California 92021, are published by Zondervan Publishing House, 5300 Patterson, S.E., Grand Rapids, Michigan 49530

Library of Congress Cataloging-in-Publication Data

McCollam, Dan, 1962-
    More junior high game nights : more wild and crazy outreach
    events for junior high ministry / Dan McCollam, Keith Betts.
        p.   cm.
    ISBN 0-310-54101-8
    1. Games. 2. Group games. 3. Amusements. 4. Youth—Recreation.
I. Betts, Keith, 1963- . II. McCollam, Dan, 1962- Junior high game nights. III. Title.
GV1201.M42 1992
793'.0192—dc20   91-17572
                                                                              CIP

Edited by Sharon Odegaard and Lory Floyd
Design and Typography by Rogers Design & Associates
Cover and interior illustrations by Corbin Hillam

Printed in the United States of America

94 95 96 97 / ML / 10 9 8 7 6 5 4

To all the teens who made discovering these ideas so much fun and so worthwhile. And to Regina and Michael for your love and patience.

CONTENTS

Preface

Many fantastic game and idea books are available for youth workers today. As youth pastors, we have used these resources and have been greatly helped by them. So what makes this collection any different—or even necessary?

Focus, first of all. These games are geared to appeal primarily to junior highers, those ages 11 to 15. Every youth worker knows that the junior higher is a totally different species. We felt it was necessary to develop a resource that was as outrageous and bizarre as the junior high mind-set (quite a challenge, huh?). *The focus of this game resource is to reach junior high teens.*

This idea book also has a different purpose. Other game books have given us great resources for building community, fellowship, and friendship through mass play and light competition. *The purpose of this book is to give you a resource that will draw in a mass of unsaved or unreached teens.* Each game has only a few actual competitors. The rest of the teens form a team of cheering spectators. This changes the whole nature of the games. The games have to be fun to watch as well as fun to play. There is a special concentration on costuming and staging because of the value of the visual entertainment.

The emphasis of these games is also quite different. Over the last few years, there has been a huge upsurge in the popularity of teen game shows, all of which share a few common denominators. First of all, we saw that contemporary props, lighting, and sound were important. Right away we put up stage lighting and a killer sound system. We saw an immediate change as each game was brightly lit and accompanied by driving Christian music. The teens were pulled right into the games.

Second, we saw the importance of crowd response. We encouraged the teens to shout, scream, and cheer for the contestants during the games. The teens immediately began to respond like a studio audience, enjoying each game right along with the competitors and yet settling down to a quiet anticipation between each competition.

Third, we noticed that the games centered more on making a mess than on athletic skill. We developed wild and messy games that were heavy on competition but low on skill. Several of these games focus on eating contests because they are messy and something that everyone is good at. Other competitions are so bizarre that everyone competes on an even level because no one has any prior experience at the game challenge.

We found that these changes in emphasis brought a huge positive response from the teens. No longer were we trying to coax teens to participate; literally hundreds of kids were lining the stage shouting, "Pick me! Pick me!" The teens were starting to have fun!

Finally, this resource has a bottom line of reaching lost souls. After all, the challenge of youth ministry is not to get teens in or to keep them in, but to see them burst into new life through personal faith in Jesus Christ. For this reason, we developed an evangelistic message for each night that goes along with the theme. We found that the games created a real willingness to hear what needs to be said and that they were effective as an evangelistic outreach.

It is our hope that this resource will be a blessing to you, and that you will find it innovative, helpful, and refreshing. Our sincere desire is that, as you use it, many souls will be won to the kingdom of God through the foolishness of man. Have fun!

SECTION ONE

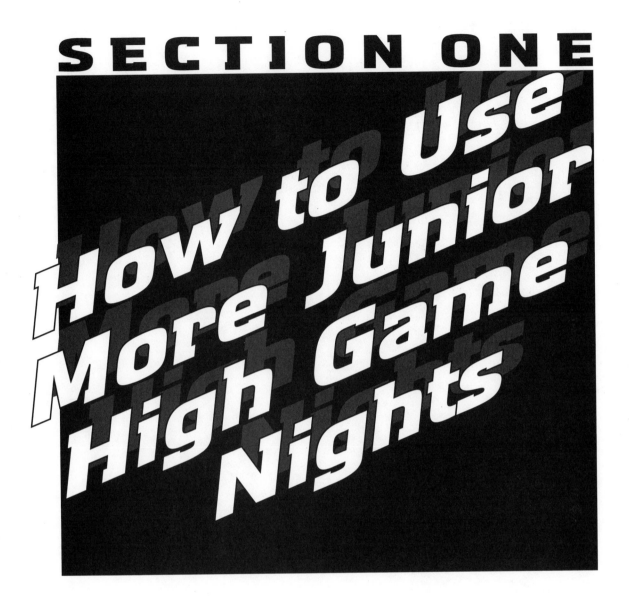

How to Use More Junior High Game Nights

Why Games?

This is the question that we asked five years ago when God led us to start an outreach program among junior high young people using creative gaming. We were hesitant because it all sounded so social and unspiritual, but God knows best. In these past years, our little youth group of 30 teenagers has reached out to well over 1,000 teens. More than 100 of these teens are beginning to join themselves to the group through a new relationship with Jesus Christ. Through this experience, God gave us the answer to the question, "Why games?" Here is what we found.

First of all, we found that games meet a genuine need. The Scriptures make it very clear that Christianity must not just preach doctrine, but it should really seek to meet a person's needs. Teens in our culture today are starving for good and wholesome activities in a positive environment. There is so little in the world today that is fun and yet truly wholesome and helpful. If these were starving natives, I would attempt to feed them; if they were naked, I would clothe them; if they were in prison, I would visit them. I would try to meet their needs so that they could meet Jesus. It became obvious to us that our teens were bored and had a legitimate need that had to be met before we would be heard as messengers of the Gospel.

Second, games tear down walls. So often kids come into youth bound by troubles and cares. Many of the teens that we work with carry a large responsibility in caring for the needs of their broken families. There is so much on these teens' minds that often it is hard to get through to them no matter how dynamic the speaker. We have found that good gaming tears down emotional walls by helping teens to laugh, to cheer, to let out screams, and that somehow then they are ready to hear. They are freed to respond to and finally receive the same truths that we have been sharing all along.

Finally, games open the door to share the Gospel with teens. We have seen kids come to game nights who would never respond to any of our other invitations. Now that they have come in the door and responded to the message, they are making the choice themselves to attend our teen teaching and worship services. Of course the game nights could never be the sole program. The wild activities give us the opportunity to get a foot in the door, to meet the teens and their families, and to speak truth into their lives. The games are just a means to an end. The goal is to share Jesus.

Why games? Because teens are ruining their lives out of boredom and silent despair, and games give them something to do that is good, clean fun in a healthy environment. Why games? Because games tear down emotional walls that help kids to hear with a fresh positive attentiveness. Why games? Because games bring in teens who otherwise might never hear a gospel that they could relate to and respond to. We have been commissioned to go out to the highways and byways and to compel them (give them a reason and a way) to come in. Good creative gaming provides opportunities to do this.

Four Keys to Successful Game Nights

The youth groups that have used this resource are reporting explosive growth in their youth outreach! You may ask, "Can we really pull off a great game night that will reach junior high teens?" We are seeing it happen again and again. All the information you will need for 12

great game nights is in this book. With the four keys of *information, invitation, preparation,* and *operation,* you will be able to hold your own great game nights and see explosive growth in your outreach.

Now that you have the *information* in this book, the next important step is *inviting* the teens. Now is the time to get the word out. These game nights have proved most effective in reaching kids 11 to 15, so the most obvious place to get the word out is in your local junior high school. We have used neon flyers with great artwork, fast moving colorful video spots, and organized team efforts. Although all of these contributed to attracting the teens, there is still nothing quite as effective as teens telling teens. Get your kids excited about it and the word will get out.

The third important key is *preparation.* Make sure you are prepared for the crowds that will respond to this type of activity. Once you have begun an outreach of this nature, you will be responsible for having enough workers to conduct the meeting in a safe and orderly manner, to run sound and lights, to help with prop construction, to help with nightly cleanup, and to administer an effective follow-up program. Don't throw out the bait unless you have built a net to catch those who come in. Your net should include workers, a follow-up program, and prayer.

The final key is *operation.* These game nights are programmed for 90-minute, fast-action meetings. We encourage you to open each meeting with a hearty welcome. Reinforce the theme in your introduction and award points or prizes for great costumes or team spirit. Briefly inform the teens about how the games will be conducted and any house rules that will help the operation run safely and effectively. Perhaps you would say, "We have so much fun planned for tonight that we are afraid we won't be able to do it all unless you help us out by following a few simple rules."

Jump right into the first game and choose your volunteers. Call up these contestants to the stage and explain the game as props are set in place by stage helpers. When the game starts, have your sound technician play some loud Christian music to get the kids excited. Encourage the crowd to shout, scream, and cheer on their teammates. After the games, have workers escort the players to a cleanup area. Stage hands should do a fast cleanup of the stage area while you introduce and choose contestants for the next challenge. Each game should run about ten minutes—from the time you introduce the game and choose the volunteers, to the operation and cleanup of the game. That means that the games portion of your program should run about 60 minutes.

At the end of the games portion, you may want to take an offering or hold a Pass-the-Buck Contest in which each team tries to get as much money in the bucket as it can during the length of one song. After the offering, you can have drama, special songs, or testimonies that go along with the night's theme. Leave yourself the last 15 to 20 minutes to present the short Gospel message provided with each game night. Conclude your message with an opportunity for response. Dismiss the kids as close to the 90-minute time mark as possible to keep things clicking. Highlight some of the features of your next game night and encourage everyone to bring friends.

Now you have everything you need to pull off a great game night. Invite your senior high youth and sponsors to be the workers who help conduct the program.

Remind them that their involvement is making a difference in teens' lives. Together you can use the information, the invitation, the preparation, and the operation to make a huge impact on your junior high school and community. Meanwhile, you just may have the best time of your life doing it!

A Note to Small Youth Groups

Don't shut out *More Junior High Game Nights*! You may look at the games in this book and say to yourself, "That is just for big crowds and big churches." Remember that this game program is meant to draw in unsaved teens. Don't look at the number in your youth group; those kids can be your worker core. Look at the number of kids in your local junior high school. This is the group you will be drawing from.

If targeting your junior high school does not seem like it would work, challenge another youth group in the area. Combine resources and choose the facility that lends itself best to this kind of program. Challenge several other church groups and ask them to share in the preaching at the end. Remind them that the only message that will ever be preached is the Gospel of the Lord Jesus Christ. Ask several churches in the area to join with you for one semester or a monthly rally. Then plan for the best in outrageous and messy excitement!

If there are no other churches that are able to join with you, check with other youth-oriented community groups. Challenge a YMCA/YWCA group, a scout troop, or a Big Brother/Big Sister program. One year we had two teams from such community groups. One group was a government runaway shelter and the other was a safe-place shelter for families in trouble. One social worker who was not a Christian gave us one of the highest recommendations that we received that year!

No matter what sources you draw from, ideas from *More Junior High Game Nights* will draw a crowd! So don't shut out the opportunity to bring hundreds of bored, troubled, needy, lonely teens into your church or gymnasium for quite possibly the best time they will ever have as teenagers. This program is for you!

"But It Sounds Involved and Expensive!"

Good news! The hardest part has already been done for you. All the games you will need are provided for each night. The theme is the thread of continuity that keeps things running smoothly and allows you to decorate and plan staging and costumes to add excitement to each night.

Props are an important part of each game night because they really add to the visual excitement. All the props in this book can be made inexpensively out of materials that can be purchased at any local toy, novelty, or hardware store. We spent about $30 per game night for props and all this expense was recovered through an offering.

If you are stranded in the boondocks where these supplies are just not available, then fear not! All of the items in this book can be ordered through toy and novelty catalogs. Since all the props are listed in the book, you can order them in advance. The discount you will get by ordering factory direct can also more than make up for any shipping costs. Our experience has been that these companies provide fast, efficient service with no back orders. They even have 1-800 numbers and overnight express.

As far as being involved, yes, it takes some work to pull off a great game night. But this book gives you a head start. You choose the night that is best for you. Monday night was an extremely effective night for us because there were few schedule conflicts and teens are generally bored on Monday nights. We found that by holding our game nights on Mondays, school attendance actually went up on Mondays in the public school! Instead of being the dreaded "Blue Monday" for many teens, it was actually the highlight of their week.

We have created 12 game nights that will work weekly, monthly, or even just occasionally. This book was created to serve you—you decide how to make the program fit your situation and your kids.

"What About the Starving Children?"

"There are an awful lot of food games. Don't you know there are starving children in Africa?" We have great compassion toward the world hunger effort. We also realize that there are teens on every block in America who are starving. Their bellies may be full, but their hearts are very empty. In this "couch potato" generation, fewer kids are athletic than ever before. Because of the collapse of the traditional family, teenagers also face an epidemic of inferiority. For some kids, the only contest that they could ever win may be an eating contest. You should see the smile that comes across a chubby little teen's face as he wins a contest for his team. Christianity meets the total need of humanity; feed all the hungry, but don't write off the food games.

As far as the hunger outreach goes, every year our game program sponsors a "Get Your Can to (Program Name) Night." To get in the building that night, the teens must all bring canned goods.

We award points to the team that brings in the most cans. Included in the games are can-stacking contests and mystery-can eating games in which the labels are peeled off and the contestant must eat whatever is inside. One year we were able to supply each of 80 families with three grocery bags stuffed with food at Thanksgiving time. For most of these families, it was the only way they could have celebrated the Thanksgiving holiday.

Tips on Trashing Your Church

"How do you get away with making such a mess of the church?" We have a great head pastor who has allowed us to do whatever it takes to win other teens to Jesus. But there are some precautions that you can take.

1. Cover your stage or play area with tarps or drop cloths and tape or fasten them down each week. Check with hardware stores or tent and awning companies for a good, heavy polyvinyl tarp that will last you through the year. This protection is well worth the initial investment and will protect your floor or carpet from any damage.

2. Choose a location that has bathrooms or changing rooms directly off the stage area. When teens finish a messy competition, don't allow them to walk out into the audience; escort them directly to these cleanup areas.

3. Assign two or three teens to be stagehands for the entire semester. Their job is to hustle tables, chairs, and other props on and off stage and to clean up after each contest. If there is a cleanup crew clearing the stage while you announce the next stunt, then the overall mess is kept under better control.

4. The slogan for our game nights was "Dress for the mess!" This prepared teens for the nature of the games and protected us from any accusations of damage to their clothes. We found this also served the purpose of breaking down fashion cliques, since no one was wearing labels—everyone was just in old jeans and T-shirts.

If your church does not have a facility suitable for such a program, check into renting or borrowing a hall or gymnasium on a regular basis. One summer, we ran the program outside in a tent on the church grounds. This also was a great success. Don't give up if you can't have it in your church; there is a place in your community where you can make it work.

Costumes, Embarrassment, and Coming Back

"You talk a lot about costumes. What's the deal?" Believe it or not, we found that teens still love to dress up. Every week included a Costume Contest in which we would award extra points to those who dressed for the theme. Dressing for the theme also helped the kids to get into the program before they ever got there. They were so excited about their costumes that we could have done just about anything and they would have loved it because their hearts were already into it.

Costume and prop suggestions are provided for each theme. The value of costumes is amazing. We have all seen the old pie-eating contest done with no hands. It's funny, but it isn't anything new. Several of the games in this book are just a twist on an old theme: you put a bunch of plastic pig noses on your contestants and suddenly the pie contest becomes a pigging out contest and everyone looks silly before they ever get started. It adds to the fun, it adds to the humor, and it gives kids a mask to hide behind that can actually make them feel more comfortable.

"Yeah, but don't you embarrass teens?" Junior high teens are already embarrassed. They are the victims of puberty and it is playing some pretty dirty tricks on them. Games like these and the crazy costumes help teens to laugh at themselves. With all the hype, the cheering, the clapping, and the shouting, we encourage each teen contestant. In this way, teens are both laughing at themselves and affirming one another. That is why we encourage you to hold a rowdy, flashy, prop-filled night of fun!

"Do teens come back when the games are over?" Great nights are definitely not a cure-all. As a matter of fact, these programs are just seeds. Scripture tells us that the Gospel is a seed. What happens to that seed after it has been sown depends on many variables. What we have tried to do is make game nights one of the best memories that a teen will ever have. Later, when that teen is hurting and in trouble, we believe that he or she will remember that the happiest time was in church. Teens will remember the people who went out of their way to show them a good, fun time. Our goal is to provide you with a seed that can bring a great harvest in your community.

To Preach or Not to Preach?

Don't be afraid to preach and don't settle for just drawing a crowd! Give teens something that they can take home. Preach the Gospel. If you get off on issues, then your game night has ceased to be an evangelistic outreach. For each game night we have provided an evangelistic message. We believe the games are tempting enough to bring back a crowd and we believe that the Gospel is the power of God unto salvation! Preach the

Word with boldness, clarity, and simplicity, and expect great results.

Working It Into Your Calendar

More Junior High Game Nights can be used effectively on a weekly, monthly, or quarterly basis. There are benefits to each calendar choice. Obviously, quarterly game nights allow you the most time to prepare, promote, follow up, and sometimes recover. This may be the best choice for a volunteer or part-time youth worker. The quarterly calendar choice also allows you the time to do these events on a larger scale. You may want to bring in a guest speaker or artist; or you may want to combine this with an existing quarterly rally or sectional rally. In selecting the quarterly choice, you have in this volume three years of the wildest tried-and-true gaming ideas for reaching junior high teens, and the time and resources to execute them with excellence!

More Junior High Game Nights also works great as part of a monthly program. Teens like the security of a routine and it gives them something to look forward to. The monthly choice allows you the time to advertise in monthly newsletters and magazines and to use your "Coming-This-Month" clip art. Perhaps the greatest advantage of the monthly choice is that it gives you a regular fun event that boosts your attendance and reaches out to the lost without interrupting your regular weekly activities. This choice means you have one full year of great gaming ideas in this volume.

The weekly choice is for kamikaze youth workers, like us, who like to have a million things going at once. "Never give them time to say, 'I'm bored'" is our motto. You will find that *More Junior High Game Nights* is complete enough to supply all you need to pull off these games on a weekly basis with only minimal brain damage. For those of you who choose this calendar option, we have several suggestions:

1. Get plenty of help from youth sponsors, volunteers, and your key teens.

2. You may want to use a cohost to help you keep things running smoothly onstage. This cohost can also share in many of the preparation responsibilities.

3. Remember to balance your program with other activities, such as opportunities for follow-up, Bible study, one-on-one, and worship.

4. Divide your game nights into six- to nine-week semesters with breaks in between to regroup, revive, recover, and refocus.

5. Buy the family-size aspirin bottle at your local supermarket.

6. Pay special attention to our suggestions in Chapter 13, Super Special Events. Here we add six game night "twists" that will open new, sizzling possiblities for alternate game night themes.

You may want to run your semesters concurrent with the school year, leaving ample time off for spring break and holiday seasons. The weekly calendar choice offers dynamic growth, high momentum, and an explosive impact on the community.

SECTION TWO

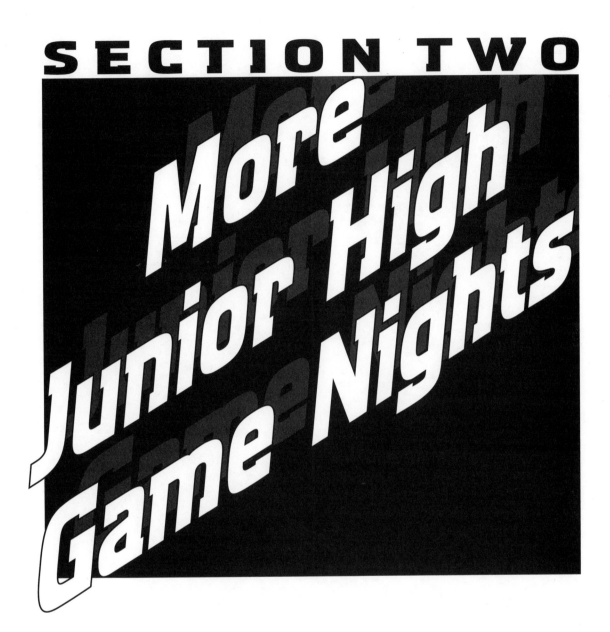

More Junior High Game Nights

1. The Mad Hatter

COSTUMES, PROPS, AND PROMOTION

Costumes: Invite all the teams to create and wear their own hats in a Weird Hat Contest. You'll be amazed what teens will come up with. Award bonus points to any team with 100 percent participation.

Props: Everything you use for this game night will start with a hat. You can purchase several plastic army helmets from a local toy store for under two dollars each. These provide a sturdy base to attach things to in a size that fits almost any kid's head. You may want to decorate the back wall with different kinds of hats. Streamers and balloons fit any occasion and add extra life to any game night. Place all your hat props on the stage to increase interest as they come in.

Promotion: Money talks. It really doesn't matter if it is a little or a lot, but offer a cash reward for the person who brings in the weirdest hat. Have some judges ready to help you decide on a winner or judge by crowd response, and do the judging before the games begin so the teens won't damage their entries. The Weird Hat Contest always goes over big!

B-BALL HELMETS

Materials:

Attach one small Nerf hoop to each of the splash helmets. Nerf hoops have suction cups that will hold them to the helmets. Supply each team with a bag of marshmallows.

The Challenge:

Choose two players from each team and stand them about six feet apart. One player wears the helmet and the other tosses the marshmallows. At the signal, catchers stick out their tongues, and tossers try to shoot marshmallows through the hoops and onto the tongues of their teammates. The first team with a player to catch a marshmallow on his or her tongue after it has passed through the hoop is the winner.

EGG HOODS

Materials:

Each contestant needs a dozen eggs and a nylon jacket or Windbreaker with a hood. For cleanup purposes, it is best if the hood unzips from the jacket.

The Challenge:

Have each contestant wear the jacket like a straitjacket: The back of the coat is worn against the chest and the arms are put through the opposite armholes. This leaves the hood of the jacket right in front of the contestant's face. Choose a second contestant to toss eggs.

At the signal, nonjacketed players toss eggs to their partners, who try to catch the eggs in the hoods of their jackets. Catchers may use their hands to hold the hoods open and position themselves under the eggs. The team to catch the most eggs in the hood is the winner. (After play, the hoods should be unzipped from the jackets while the catchers are still wearing them. This prevents further mess, as eggs may be dumped out and hoods thrown in a washing machine.)

GIANT CANDLE HATS

Materials:

You need one candlestick and one two-inch candlestick holder for each contestant. Place the candle in the candlestick, then stick the candlestick through the center of a felt or a cardboard top hat. When the hat is put on, the candlestick holder will rest on the player's head. Arm each contestant with a squirt bottle or water cannon.

The Challenge:

Seat the players in a circle, each armed with a squirt bottle and a candle hat. Light all the candle hats. At the signal, players try to extinguish their opponents' flames with their squirt bottles. When a player's candle goes out, the teen must cease fire and leave the circle. The last player lit is the winner.

SPLASH HELMETS

Materials:

Create one splash helmet for each contestant as follows: Purchase a toy army helmet from your local toy store. Punch a large nail or screw through the center of the helmet so that the point sticks out the top. It's best if these helmets can be strapped to the players' heads using the factory strap or by adding an eight-inch long piece of quarter-inch elastic to the bottom sides of the helmet. Fill a six-inch water balloon half full of water and half full of air. Tie the balloon to the nail or screw with a 12-inch piece of cord or string.

The Challenge:

Strap a splash helmet onto each contestant's head. At the signal, players begin to throw their bodies and wiggle their heads in an attempt to pop the water balloons on the spikes sticking out of their helmets. The first player to pop the balloon on his or her own spike is the winner.

THIEF THUMPERS

Materials:

Each contestant needs a new toilet scrubber and a ski mask or old pair of nylons. Fill one water balloon for each player.

The Challenge:

Have contestants place the water balloons on their heads and then pull the ski masks or nylons down over their heads. Arm each thief with a toilet scrubber. At the signal, players thump each other on the head with the toilet scrubbers, attempting to pop the water balloons. Each player is trying to burst the balloons of the opponents while keeping his or her own from being popped. The last thief with an unpopped balloon is the winner.

Materials:

Purchase a two-liter bottle of soft drink and a toy army helmet for each contestant. Remove the plastic pedestal bottoms from all the two-liter bottles. Construct an ultimate party hat for each contestant using the two-liter bottles, the pedestal bottoms, the helmets, some nuts and bolts, and some thin plastic tubing. For each party hat, you need about four feet of quarter-inch tubing, which may be purchased inexpensively from a local hardware store.

Bolt the pedestal bottom to the top of the army helmet. Using a nail, poke a small hole just below the neck of the two-liter bottle. The hole should be just big enough so that the plastic tubing fits through snugly. Insert the four-foot tube into the hole until the tubing reaches the bottom of the two-liter bottle. Place the torpedo shaped two-liter bottle firmly into its pedestal on top of the army helmet. You now have an ultimate party hat.

The Challenge:

Introduce your creation like this: "I'm sure you have all seen the drinker's party hat at stores. It is a ball cap with a plastic pedestal to hold two cans of your favorite drink. The hat has two straw tubes coming down to the mouth so both cans can be sipped at the same time. The advent of the Big Gulp, the Guzzler, and other large capacity soft drinks show America's increasing demand for more soda. Well, tonight we are going to present you with the ultimate party hat and the ultimate soft drink container!"

Call up contestants from each team and strap the helmets to their heads. At the signal, players begin to sip down the soda. When the suction starts, it probably won't stop, which adds to the humor as teens try to control the steady flow of the soft drinks. You may want to allow them to tag off with a friend. The first team to drain its party hat is the winner.

TONIGHT'S MESSAGE: HIDING BEHIND A HAT

Introduction:

We can tell a lot about what a person does by the hat he or she wears. (You may want to hold up some different hats and have the teens identify what the wearer does. Do this with a bit of humor so as not to insult their intelligence.) One thing you can't tell from a hat is what a person is like on the inside.

Focus:

Sometimes we hide behind hats or images of what people think of us, and we are really something very different on the inside. Tonight we are going to talk about *hats people hide behind.*

1. The hat of achievement. A lot of people hide behind what they can do— what they can or will achieve. The only problem with this hat is that when the achievement is gone, this person holds only a lifeless memory that can lead to feelings of loneliness and failure. **Life does not depend on what we can do.**

2. The hat of reputation. Many people live only for what others think of them. This is an exhausting lifestyle, since you end up a slave to everyone you meet. You spend your whole life painting a picture of someone you are not, changing yourself to suit the ideas of people you don't even respect. **Life does not depend on what others think of us.**

3. The hat of failure. Some people hide behind a hat of failure. These people may have made a mistake somewhere in life and judge all other things by that one mistake. They feel that they can never fit in and never be good at anything. By doing this, they excuse themselves from trying. **Life does not depend on past success or failure.**

Conclusion:

So what does life depend on? It depends on who we really are on the inside. What we are on the inside depends on who we are in Christ. In Christ, we can be free from finding significance only in what we can do or in what others think of us and from measuring our whole lives on yesterday's success or failure. Tonight, are you hiding behind a hat? Come to Christ. He is the answer.

2. Alien Adventure

COSTUMES, PROPS, AND PROMOTION

Costumes: Hold an Alien Costume Contest. Teens dress up as a favorite television alien or invent their own. You may want to offer a prize or cash incentive for the best costume. Award team points for best participation.

Props: Have some of your more artistic teens make a giant flying saucer using cardboard, aluminum foil, and paints.

You may even want to hook up some flashing Christmas lights to your flying saucer for special effects. Hang the saucer on the wall behind your stage as decoration or outside your building as advertising. Place all game props on the stage before the teens enter to increase interest as they arrive.

Promotion: This event is really fun to

advertise. Get your teens to start a rumor about UFOs being sighted around the church. Have them dress in alien costumes and pass out flyers after school. Put up posters that say, "They're Coming! Alien Adventure! (date, place, and time)." Don't give much information on the poster, just enough to spark some interest. You may even have a Flying Saucer Contest in which kids decorate their cars like spaceships. Have fun with this one!

E.T. EATERS

Materials:

Supply each contestant with a bowl of M&M's candies and a pair of tube socks with two small finger holes cut in the toes.

The Challenge:

Players place the tube socks over their hands so that only their index and middle fingers are sticking out the holes. Seat the players at a table with the bowls of candy in front of them. At the signal, players eat E.T.-style, using only the fingers that are sticking out of the socks. The first player to finish off his or her candy is the winner.

FLYING SAUCERS

Materials:

Each team needs a net bag or shopping bag with two hooped handles, a stack of 12 paper dessert plates or saucers, and a can of shaving cream.

The Challenge:

Choose three players from each team. Two of these players each place one handle of the shopping bag around their necks so that the bag rests between them. At the signal, the third player fills the 12 paper dessert plates or saucers with shaving cream and tosses them toward the bag. The team to catch the most flying saucers in the bag wins.

MORK SHUTTLE

Materials:

Supply each team with one dozen eggs and a medium sized mixing bowl.

The Challenge:

Before play begins, remind the teens how Mork thought all eggs were spaceships. Choose two players from each team, one to be Mork (the tosser) and the other to be a landing pad. Have the players who are landing pads lie down on their bellies and set the mixing bowls on their backs. Position the tossers ten to 12 feet away.

At the signal, tossers launch their eggs, trying to land them in the bowls on their partners' landing pads. The team to land the most eggs in the bowl is the winner.

PHONE HOME

Materials:

Run a speaker telephone into your auditorium and mike it so that everyone can hear your phone calls. Your local telephone company may also have a telephone or attachment that will hook directly into your PA system.

The Challenge:

Remember how E.T. was always trying to phone home? Announce that tonight you are going to phone the teens' homes and ask whoever answers to describe what the teen was wearing when he or she left home. Make sure to call the homes of those in costume. When you call, announce that you are from the church so that no one will think it is a kidnapping or prank call. If the person on the other end of the line can describe the teen's costume, award that team points. Award extra points for the team that gets the most creative or detailed description of what a teen was wearing. This game is always full of laughs!

TAKE ME TO YOUR LITER

Materials:

Each team needs one two-liter bottle of soft drink and one box of small Dixie cups.

The Challenge:

Choose one leader for each team to hold and pour the two-liter bottle of soft drink. At the signal, players run one at a time to their leaders, holding the cups with their teeth. The leaders fill the cups with a few ounces of soft drink that the players must drink through their teeth without touching the cups with their hands. When a player finishes the soft drink, he or she runs back to the team to tag off with another player. Everyone gets a free drink and everyone gets drenched. The first team to empty its two-liter bottle wins.

UNIDENTIFIED FLYING OBJECTS

Materials:

You need one bucket of "UFOs" and one target for each team. Your UFO can be any unidentified flying object, but one idea is buckets of mashed potatoes dyed in different team colors. Make sure your UFO or potatoes will stick to the targets. Make the triangle targets on four-by-eight-foot sheets of plywood with paint or colored tape.

The Challenge:

Players line up about eight feet from their targets. At the signal, players scoop out their potatoes and hurl them toward the target boards. Remember to place extra tarps under and behind the targets. The first team to cover its triangle target with UFOs is the winner. Have fun with this one!

TONIGHT'S MESSAGE: NOT OF THIS WORLD

Scripture: John 18:36-37.

Hint:

You may want to play Petra's "Not of This World" or Larry Norman's "Unidentified Flying Object" before speaking.

Introduction:

If this Scripture is true, then a Christian should be as different as an alien walking down a city street.

Focus:

Tonight we want to speak on *three differences every Christian who is not of this world should have.*

1. The difference of language. Christians should speak a different language from that of the world. Ephesians 4:29 warns us not to let any unwholesome talk come out of our mouths, but only what is helpful for building others up according to their needs. That means Christians should not engage in cutdowns, dirty jokes, slander, backbiting, and the like, but should only encourage other people.

2. The difference of lifestyle. Can you imagine an alien coming up to interview a person smoking a cigarette or doing drugs? Here is what I picture happening.

Alien: What's that?
Earthling: Oh, this? It's a cigarette.
Alien: What are you doing to it?
Earthling: I'm smoking it. What do you think I'm doing with it?
Alien: Does it taste good?
Earthling: No, actually it tastes terrible.
Alien: Well, is it like medicine? Is it helping you?
Earthling: No, actually it is killing me.
Alien: Well, is someone forcing you to do this?
Earthling: No, I do it for kicks.

Sin and corruptible habits should be that foreign to a Christian. Christians should have a different focus and a different purpose in life that will be reflected in their lifestyles. See Ephesians 5.

3. The difference of destination. An alien has a different home. We are not to store up treasures for ourselves here on earth because we don't plan on living here forever. Heaven is our home. Here we are strangers and aliens.

Conclusion:

If we live as the world does and share in its corruption, we will also share in its judgment. Every Christian should be an alien of this world in language, lifestyle, and destination. In which world are you?

3. Sports Spectacular

COSTUMES, PROPS, AND PROMOTION

Costumes: Invite teens to attend in any appropriate sports uniform. Teens may also bring sports equipment from home for bonus team spirit. Announce that bonus points will be given to the team with the largest variety of sporting equipment.

Props: Use a referee's whistle as the starting signal for each game. Game props should be sufficient to decorate the stage. Place all the game props on the stage in advance to increase interest as the teens come in.

Promotion: This is a great opportunity to invite in a Christian professional athlete. Since you are not limited to one sport, you should be able to find a professional or hometown hero who is willing to speak to your group. Promote your guest at local schools and be sure to inform school coaches who may want their entire team to hear your guest speaker. This is also a great opportunity to honor a church team or, better yet, a school team, with a trophy. Invite the whole team out to a special recognition night. The Sports Spectacular also gives you an opportunity to show a short bloopers movie. Play it while the teens are coming in or just before you speak to get the teens' full attention.

BACKWARD BANANA BATON RELAY

Materials:

Each team needs four bananas and four runners.

The Challenge:

Have the runners stand at the four corners of their teams. Runners hold half-peeled bananas on their heads with both hands, with the peeled portion facing backward. At the signal, the first-leg runner on each team runs backward to the hand-off runner. That runner must eat the first runner's banana down to the peel while keeping his or her own banana firmly overhead. Once the banana has been eaten, the runner races to the next hand-off position. Play continues until the last player crosses the finish line and hands his or her banana to a nonrunner. The first team to polish off four bananas and finish the race is the winner.

BASEBALL BASH

Materials:

Supply each team with a large Whiffle bat, three small water balloons, and a home plate.

The Challenge:

Have a batter stand over the plate with the Whiffle bat. Each batter will get three pitches. When the Whiffle bat connects with the water balloon, there is usually quite a spray of water over the audience. Each balloon that explodes scores one home run. A balloon that is hit but doesn't explode is equal to a double with a ghost runner rotation. That means that two hits in a row that do not burst would score one run with a man on second. Three hits that do not burst would score two runs and leave one man on second. Players bat until all three balloons have been hit. Runs are totaled and a winner is announced. Save a few balloons for a tiebreaker.

BOP BOXING

Materials:

For this game, you need two chairs, two baseball caps, and several punch balloons. (Punch balloons are eighteen-inch balloons with large rubber bands attached. They are sold under a variety of names at your local toy stores and drugstores.)

The Challenge:

Seat two contestants directly across from one another in folding chairs. Have them adjust their caps to fit tightly on their heads. Each boxer must sit on one hand while firmly grasping the punch balloon in the other hand.

When the whistle sounds the beginning of the bout, players begin to swing their balloons toward their opponents, attempting to knock off their ball caps. Make sure that the boxers are seated a little more than an arm's distance from each other so that only their balloons make contact. The first player to knock off the other player's hat is the winner by K.O.—that's "knock off!"

FOOTBALL REACTIONARY TRAINING DRILL

Materials:

All you need for this gag is two folding chairs, a bucket of water, and a large sponge. Make sure you choose regulars who are known as good sports for your contestants.

The Challenge:

Announce that you want to check the reaction time of your football players. Set two folding chairs about four feet apart, facing each other. You will sit in one chair and the contestant in the other. Send the other contestants out of the room. Explain that you want the player to imitate everything you do as fast as he can.

Start play by jumping to your feet and shouting, "Ugh!" The contestant is to imitate you as quickly and forcefully as possible. Now quickly move your hands in a downward motion yelling, "Ugh!" Again, the contestant should imitate you. Then move your hands right to left and up and down, preceding each command with a loud, "Ugh!" Call commands faster and louder each time.

While the player is watching you closely and imitating your movements, continue giving distracting commands as someone slips a wet sponge on the contestant's folding chair. With one last "Ugh!" sit down in your chair. The contestant reacts to your motion and sits on the wet sponge, spraying water everywhere and sending the crowd into a roar of laughter. Shake the player's hand, and have the crowd give him a round of applause. Award him points, then dry off the seat and call in your next contestant.

POOL VAULTING

Materials:

You need three or four inflatable children's swimming pools. Fill each pool with water, shaving cream, eggs, or your favorite slime.

The Challenge:

Choose some contestants who consider themselves good jumpers. Place two of the pools in a line. At the signal, each player tries to qualify by jumping *over* the two swimming pools. When all the players have qualified, add another swimming pool. When a player misses and lands in a pool, he or she is disqualified. Add another pool after each round. The player with the longest pool vault is the winner.

WHEATIES EATIES

Materials:

You need one large box of Wheaties for every two players. Supply each contestant with a large mixing bowl and a large serving spoon.

The Challenge:

Announce that, of course, Wheaties is considered the breakfast of champions and that to get tonight's Sports Spectacular off to a good start, you will have a Wheaties Eaties Contest. Seat your volunteers at a table. Bring out the giant bowls of Wheaties, give each player a spoon, and pour on the milk. Start the contest with a whistle and stand back. The first player to finish a bowl of Wheaties is the winner.

TONIGHT'S MESSAGE: TRAINING FOR TRIUMPH

Scripture: 1 Timothy 4:7-8.

Introduction:

Everyone seems concerned with physical training these days. Television is flooded with commercials for exercise centers and bodybuilding clubs. This Scripture tells us that physical training is good, but training in godliness is even better.

Focus:

Tonight we are going to share *the ben-* *efits of training for godliness.*

1. Promise for this life. Godliness is not just for someday when we go to heaven. A godly life is a happy life. All the beatitudes begin with the word *blessed.* That word means truly happy, having the kind of contagious Christianity that others want. Godliness is not just to gain entrance into heaven— it is also the key to the most enjoyable life on this earth.

2. Promise for the world to come. While we are rejoicing in the benefits of godliness now, we cannot miss out on the supreme benefits of the world to come. Heaven is not just a place where we will float around, sit on clouds, and play harps. God has prepared a new heaven and a new earth where righteousness will dwell.

Conclusion:

To practice godliness is to enjoy the best of life now and to store up treasures in heaven. Don't think that to live for God now is to lose all enjoyment in this life and to gain only future blessing. Perhaps this is what has kept you from giving your life to Jesus. Come now and train for triumph!

4. Caveman Night

COSTUMES, PROPS, AND PROMOTION

Costumes: Invite teens to dress up in caveman costume, or have a Missing Link Look-alike Contest. For bonus points, have a Boulder Bash in which the person to carry in the biggest rock wins extra points or a prize. You may also want to begin the program with a Rock Concert. Have every team member bring two rocks, and award bonus points to the team that makes the most noise by banging its rocks together.

Props: An impressive stage prop for this theme is an inflatable dinosaur, available at your local toy store. Some inflate up to eight feet in height. You may want to construct a huge cave by shaping chicken wire and covering it with material or papier-maché. Check your church prop room for an Easter tomb from the last pageant, as this makes an ideal cave prop.

Promotion: This is a great week to send out a "missed you" letter to teens who have not recently attended. Your letter could say, "Come to Caveman Night! Great games! Great fun! You are the missing link!" You may want to award the inflatable dinosaur or a stuffed Dino doll to the person who brings in the most "missing links."

BATTLE OF THE TAR PITS

Materials:

Bring in a long tug-of-war rope and a small, inflatable swimming pool. Inflate the pool and fill it with a gallon of maple syrup or some other sticky substance for your tar pit.

The Challenge:

This game is basically an old-fashioned tug-of-war, with the teams lined up on each side of the tar pit. The pool of tar gives a little added indoor excitement. The first team to pull the other team into the tar pit is the winner.

CAVE DRAWING

Materials:

For this competition you need a large chalkboard or a tripod with newsprint. Be sure to have extra chalk or markers handy. Make up some contest cards for a game of picture charades using prehistoric subjects. Examples are *dinosaur, mammoth, volcano, tar pit*, and *spear*. You will need ten subject cards for each contestant.

The Challenge:

Teams will compete one at a time. Choose one cave drawer for each team. Each team will have 90 seconds to guess as many answers as possible. At the signal, the cave drawer begins to draw pictures of the subject. Team members will shout out answers. When a correct answer is given, the drawer proceeds to the next subject card. If a correct answer is not given, the drawer may pass to the next card. The team to guess the most cave drawings in 90 seconds is the winner.

CAVE FOOD

Materials:

Supply each contestant with a paper plate full of Chef Boyardee Dinosaurs. If these are unavailable, you may want to use a bowl of Fruity Pebbles cereal.

The Challenge:

Seat the players at a table. At the signal, players eat the cave food without using their hands. The first caveman to finish his or her plate is the winner.

CAVEMAN TRIVIA

Materials:

Trivia games are still a best-seller in the game market around the country. Write up some trivia questions for *The Flintstones*, *Flintstone Babies*, *Captain Caveman*, or *Land Before Time*. Every youth group probably has at least one couch potato who should be able to supply you with some good questions. If not, a few are listed below.

1. Who was Fred Flintstone's best friend? Answer: Barney
2. What was the name of Fred's wife? Answer: Wilma
3. What was the name of Barney's wife? Answer: Betty
4. What was the name of their town? Answer: Bedrock
5. What was the name of Fred's pet? Answer: Dino
6. What was the name of Fred's boss? Answer: Mr. Slate
7. What was the name of Fred's lodge? Answer: The Loyal Order of Water Buffaloes
8. What was the name of Fred's daughter? Answer: Pebbles
9. What was the name of Barney's adopted son? Answer: Bam Bam
10. What was Fred's favorite sport? Answer: Bowling

The Challenge:

Choose one or two contestants from each team. Have the players sit in a line, one behind the other. Explain that the question is always directed to the first person in line. Each contestant has only five seconds to answer the question. If that person misses the question, he or she runs to the back of the line and everyone else advances one seat. Ask the questions quickly to try to fluster the contestant and to keep the game moving. You may want to choose some harder questions. The person in the front seat at the end of the competition or when you are all out of questions is the winner.

CAVEWOMAN RESCUE

Materials:

This activity requires one old bicycle inner tube and some black electrician's tape. Each male contestant should have a large water balloon. Make a bone head for each female contestant by piercing the center of a headband with a sharp nail or tack. When the headband is placed on the girl's head, the sharp point of the nail or tack should be straight up.

The Challenge:

Have two "cavewomen," each wearing a bone head popping device, sit in folding chairs facing each other, about 20 feet apart.

Use the electrician's tape to make two loops in the inner tube big enough to slip a foot through. Have two male contestants each slip one foot through one of the inner tube loops. The male players should now face their female teammates and draw the inner tube tight between them. Each male player is given one water balloon.

At the signal, players will try to reach their female teammates and pop the water balloons on their bone heads. With the inner tube between them, this becomes an ankle tug-of-war. The first player to pop the balloon on his teammate's head without throwing the balloon is the winner.

CLUB CLASH

Materials:

Each contestant will need a net bag or a ten-pound potato sack. Tie two rope loops to each potato sack so that one loop can hang on each shoulder. Place three to six eggs in each bag. Supply each contestant with a club. Plastic clubs may be purchased from a costume or novelty shop, or you can use a rolled up newspaper or magazine as a club.

The Challenge:

Have the volunteers slip the bags over their shoulders so that the eggs lay on their backs. Arm each contestant with a club. At the signal, players will strike their opponents' bags with their clubs to try to crush the eggs. After a few minutes of play, call for an egg check. Players whose eggs are all crushed must sit out and play continues. The last player with an egg intact is the winner.

TONIGHT'S MESSAGE: THE MISSING LINK

Introduction:

No one has ever been able to produce evidence of a species connecting man and the ape. Scientists have named this theoretical species the "missing link." It is sad that man would rather connect himself with an animal than with God. In creation there actually is no missing link.

Focus:

Tonight we will speak about *the link between God and man.*

1. The link of creation (Genesis 1:27). God created a link between God and man. He made us in his image so he could have fellowship with us. As he walked with Adam daily in the garden,

God would like to walk with each person.

2. The link was broken (Genesis 3:23-24). Man was banished from God's garden because of willful disobedience. Likewise, John 3:19 tells us that all men loved darkness rather than light, because their deeds were evil. Man broke the link between himself and God by adding the foreign ingredient of sin. Sin separates us from God.

3. Jesus restored the link (1 Timothy 2:5). For years there was a missing link between God and man. That link was restored when Jesus became the mediator between God and man. In a sense, Jesus is the only missing link there has ever been, although he was really never missing—he was just waiting for the fullness of time. Now God has again called us to fellowship with his Son, Jesus Christ our Lord (1 Corinthians 1:9).

Conclusion:

Is there a missing link in your life? If you are not having fellowship with God, there is. First John 1:6 says that if we say we have fellowship with God and yet walk in darkness, we lie and do not live by the truth. Christ gave his life to restore that missing link. Now it is up to you to claim and complete the link between you and God.

5. Fifties Flashback

COSTUMES, PROPS, AND PROMOTION

Costumes: Every teen can participate in a fifties' costume event. Refresh this young generation on what clothes were like in the fifties or some teens will show up in bell-bottom jeans, flowered shirts, and rose-colored glasses. Boys will want to wear straight-leg jeans and white T-shirts, greased hair, and leather jackets. Girls may want to wear poodle skirts and sweaters or jeans and their boyfriends' school jackets.

Props: Decorate the stage with game props for the Fifties Flashback. Many party supply stores carry a custom fifties decoration pack, complete with soda shop, Chevys, and huge rock and roll records.

Promotion: The Fifties Telephone Booth

Stuff is always a favorite. Promote this game in advance, being sure to make use of local media. The flashback idea or *Back to the Future* concept is still very popular, so you may want to work up a skit or a short drama using a time travel theme. It also lends itself to slogans such as "Get Back to the Fun!" or "Flashback to the Fifties!"

BRYLCREEM CONTEST

Materials:

Have a few towels and combs ready. You may want to invite some parents to be judges.

The Challenge:

Encourage the teens to come in costume. Most kids will roll up their jeans and grease back their hair. Choose one or two of the greasiest boys from each team. Run a different comb through each boy's hair. Have the judges examine the combs. The contestant to leave the most grease on the comb is the Brylcreem winner. Remind them that next time "a little dab'll do ya!"

GOLDFISH SWALLOWING CONTEST

Materials:

Purchase one package of Pepperidge Farm goldfish crackers for each contestant.

The Challenge:

Goldfish swallowing was a big deal in the fifties. You may want to demonstrate the actual technique with a few feeder goldfish from your local pet store. Bring your volunteers onstage and watch the relieved looks as you pull out the goldfish crackers.

Seat the players at a table and pour a large bowl of crackers for each contestant. At the signal, players begin to eat the crackers without using their hands. The first one to finish all the goldfish wins.

LIP SYNC CONTEST

Materials:

Make a master track tape for yourself of 30-second clips of old fifties songs. Record each song on your master on different tapes to give to contestants. Pass out the practice cassettes one week in advance and have the contestants practice for the Lip Sync Contest.

The Challenge:

Have each contestant perform his or her 30-second clip toward the end of the night. Build up this event as a grand finale. Judge the winner on lip sync performance, costume, and stage presence, or by crowd response.

PHONE BOOTH STUFF

Materials:

Borrow a telephone booth from a phone company or obtain one from a junkyard or a reclamation company. Some telephone companies have a portable booth they will loan out. If a telephone booth is unavailable, you may be able to make one out of a refrigerator box. Cut and paint the box to look like a phone booth.

The Challenge:

Give each team 60 seconds to get as many people in the telephone booth as possible. At the end of 60 seconds, count the people as they exit the booth one at a time. Have the crowd count along with you to add to the excitement. The team to fit the most people into the phone booth wins.

SOCK HOP

Materials:

Supply each contestant with one tube sock and one egg.

The Challenge:

Have the contestants remove their right shoes and socks. Each player pushes an egg down into the toe of the tube sock so that it sticks out beyond the toes, then puts the sock on. At the signal, players begin to hop on their right feet, trying to keep their eggs from cracking. If too much slack gets in the sock, the egg slips beneath the foot and is crushed. The last player hopping with his or her egg intact is the winner.

SODA SIPPIN' CONTEST

Materials:

Buy a two-liter bottle of root beer for each team. Pour the root beer into a pitcher with a scoop of vanilla ice cream. Place two long straws in each pitcher—the bigger the straw, the better!

The Challenge:

Choose one girl and one boy to represent each team. Have the couples sit in folding chairs facing one another as if seated at a small table. Bring out the pitchers of soda and set them on the laps of the boys. At the signal, couples begin to sip the soda as fast as possible through the straws. The first couple to finish its soda is the winner.

TONIGHT'S MESSAGE: CHANGING TIMES

Scripture: 1 Corinthians 13:13.

Introduction:

The fifties are now fondly remembered as "happy days." At that time in America, it seemed that there would be peace and prosperity for all and that things would keep getting better and better.

Times have changed. We are seeing more frequently than ever before the overturning of nations, natural disasters, and the threat of death from new strains of disease.

Focus:

Tonight we want to answer the question, *"With so many things changing, what may this generation hold on to?"*

1. We must hold on to our faith. Faith is ever-abiding in a changing universe. Our faith in God links us to the unchanging, eternal one—to something bigger than our temporal life here. We must hold to our faith to stand strong in these changing times.

2. We must hold on to hope. Some people feel that this is "the first generation without hope." With suicide as one of the major causes of death of teenagers, we know that hopelessness is a real enemy. Hope is having a personal faith in God—not just believing that God *can* do something, but that he *will* do something for you personally. Many people believe that God is able to do great things, but they have no hope that he will do so for them. This generation must hold on to the hope of God's ever-present promises found in his Word.

3. We must hold on to love. Love is the greatest of the three because Scripture says that God is love. God not only has love for us, but he is himself love. If you only *have* love, then your love may come and go, swell and fade. But when you *are* love, you can never deny yourself to one who seeks that love. Love incorporates the very character of God.

Conclusion:

In these ever-changing, unstable times, we must hold on to those things that remain: faith, hope, and love. For when all is said and done, we will find that only these really matter. Tonight, perhaps you are fearful of the threat of cancer or AIDS. Perhaps you fear the dark cloud of economic collapse that looms on the horizon. Perhaps simply not knowing what is ahead causes you to fear. You can find strength tonight in the things that last: faith, hope, and love.

6. The Egg-Stravaganza

COSTUMES, PROPS, AND PROMOTION

Costumes: Hold an Egghead Contest in which the challenge is to make your head look as much like an egg as possible. Teens may want to use wigs that look like skin and spray paint or just white face makeup. Award a prize to the best egghead look-alike.

Props: Many novelty shops sell plastic chicken beaks that add greatly to the humor of any of these games. Have each contestant wear a chicken beak during competition as part of the game props. Set up all game props on the stage before the meeting to heighten interest as the teens enter.

Promotion: This game theme works very well around Easter. You may want to add an Egg Decorating Contest in which you offer a prize or points to the teen who brings the best decorated egg. The Egg-Stravaganza also works well around spring break, using the idea of an egg hatching as breaking into fun or new life. Of course, teens never need an excuse to throw eggs and have a great time, so The Egg-Stravaganza is sure to be a hit whenever you hold it.

ANOTHER GREAT EGG TOSS

Materials:

Supply each team with two oven mitts, two swim fins, an egg or straw basket, and a dozen eggs. If swim fins are unavailable, you can use a pair of tennis shoes.

The Challenge:

Choose three contestants from each team and instruct them to stand an equal distance apart, forming a triangle. One contestant holds the egg carton with the egg basket placed at his or her feet. The second contestant wears the oven mitts, and the third contestant wears the swim fins (or tennis shoes) on his or her hands. At the signal, the first player sets an egg in play by tossing it to the second player. If the egg is caught without breaking, it is tossed to the third player. If the egg is still unbroken, it is tossed back to the first player, who places the unbroken egg in the basket. The team to deliver the most eggs safely back to the egg basket is the winner.

BASKET CASE

Materials:

Supply each team with a large Easter basket and one dozen eggs.

The Challenge:

Choose two players from each team. Teammates should face one another at a distance of about eight feet. Have one player from each team hold the Easter basket on his or her head. The other players hold the eggs. At the signal, players toss the eggs and try to land them in their partners' Easter baskets. The team with the most eggs in its basket at the end is the winner.

EGG BLAST

Materials:

You need an eight-foot section of clear plastic tubing about one inch in diameter, available at any hardware store. You also need a small funnel and one dozen eggs.

The Challenge:

Call up two volunteers with a lot of wind and strong stomachs. Have each player hold one end of the tube. While they are holding the tube, crack the egg and pour it into the tube using the funnel. At the signal, players put their mouths to the tube and begin to blow. Since the tubing is clear, everyone can see the progress of the contest. The winner is the player to blast the egg out the other side of the tube. This is one the teens will want to do again and again.

EGG DROP SOUP

Materials:

Each team needs three eggs and a small plastic cup.

The Challenge:

Choose two players from each team, one to drop the eggs and one to receive them. Have the receivers lie down on their backs and put the bottoms of the cups in their mouths. The droppers stand directly over their partners' heads, either at floor level or on folding chairs. At the signal, players crack open their eggs and try to drop the insides into the plastic cups. Give each team three tries. The team to drop the most eggs into the cup is the winner.

FIRST FEATHERS

Materials:

Each contestant will need an old feather pillow that can be ripped and popped. You may choose to use a garbage bag stuffed with any sort of feathers as a substitute for actual pillows—sometimes these work better. Feathers may be donated by a farmer, a hunter, or a meat market.

The Challenge:

A new twist to the good, old-fashioned pillow fight, the object of the game is to be the first person to pop your pillow, sending the feathers flying. At the signal, players begin a normal pillow fight, batting each other with the pillows until the feathers begin to fly. The first player to show feathers is the winner.

HATCHING THE CHECK

Materials:

Inflate one dozen ten-inch white opaque balloons for each team. Put a check for a small amount ($.50 to $5.00) into one of the balloons before inflating. You may want to place a few blank slips of paper in other balloons to throw people off. Place all the balloons in a large basket, bathtub, or inflatable swimming pool.

The Challenge:

Choose a "hen" from each team. Have the hens sit in folding chairs, which are placed an equal distance away from the balloons. At the signal, the players run from their seats to grab a balloon, then return to their seats to try to pop them. The only legal way to pop or "hatch" the eggs is by sitting on them in the folding chairs. No popping with keys or fingernails is allowed. Players may bounce, shuffle from side to side, or take running jumps for the balloons, but each balloon must be hatched with a player's seat. The first hen to hatch the check is the winner.

TONIGHT'S MESSAGE: BREAKING INTO LIFE

Introduction:

We have all seen movies of a chick breaking out of an egg. The chick must keep chipping away the shell piece by piece if it is to break into life.

Focus:

The Christian life is much like the process of a chick breaking out of an egg.

1. As the chick must chip away the hard shell, every Christian must chip away the old self (Ephesians 4:22-32). We are to put off falsehood, anger, stealing, and unwholesome talk. For many this is not an instant process but a constant chipping away at the old self. As God shows us areas where we need to change, we submit ourselves to his work of breaking down those areas of weakness in our lives.

2. As the chick needs a suitable envi-ronment for breaking out of the egg, so **every Christian needs a suitable environment to put off the old self (Hebrews 10:24-25).** You will remember that a chick must be kept in an incubator or other warm place in order to hatch from the egg. Likewise, Christians need the warmth and love of a church to help them break into new life. God knew it would be to hard to chip away the old self if we stayed constantly around those who do not have his life, so he commanded us to assemble together with other believers. In this environment we can be warmed by the presence of God's love and by the Holy Spirit, and we are spurred on to chip away at the old self.

3. As the chick breaks out of the shell and into new life, so may every Christian break out of the old self and into new life (Ephesians 4:24). Just as that chick is created in the image of its mother, so are we created in the image of the one who gave us life. Scripture says that we were created to be like God in true righteousness and holiness. It is only the shell of the old self that has hidden us from the glory of his image.

Conclusion:

Every Christian can be like the chick who chips away at the shell to break into new life. We must chip away at the old self, keep in the environment of God's love, and remember that we were created to be like God. Have you experienced the joy of putting away the old self and breaking into newness of life? You can do so tonight!

7. Back To School Bash

COSTUMES, PROPS, AND PROMOTION

Costumes: Invite teens to come out in school colors, jackets, T-shirts, or sports uniforms. Buttons, banners, and even bumper stickers should all be worth bonus points. For added fun, you may want to have a Favorite Teacher Look-alike Contest in which teens dress up like their favorite teachers.

Props: Decorate your stage area with school banners, logos, and posters. Place game props, such as blackboards and desks, on the stage in advance to add to the decor and heighten interest.

Promotion: The Back to School Bash works great as an opening night in early fall or following any holiday dismissal, such as Thanksgiving, Christmas, or spring break. Use this game night as a promotion to reach into your local junior high schools. Invite teachers, sports teams, and school officials to attend. You may want to hold a Favorite Teacher Contest in advance and invite the teacher to a short award ceremony in his or her honor at your game night. This is also a great way to get teens who love their school to come out to your game night for the first time. The concept behind the Back to School Bash is providing fun things that you just can't do in school. This night should include "Everything you wanted to do in school, but weren't allowed to." That slogan has great teen appeal.

BOMB THE DUNCE

Materials:

Each team needs a large stack of old newspapers and a dunce hat. You can make a dunce hat by rolling newspaper into a cone shape and cutting off the excess on the bottom so that it sits flat on the head.

The Challenge:

Choose one player from each team to be the dunce. While wearing the dunce hats, the players sit on stools in front of the teams. At the signal, each team wads and throws newspaper at the other team dunces, attempting to knock off their hats. All team members must stay seated during the competition. Dunces may not block shots with their hands. The last dunce with a hat on his or her head is the winner.

BUBBLE BLOWING CONTEST

Materials:

Supply each contestant with a pack of Super Bubble bubble gum. Make sure you have plenty of rulers and appoint judges to measure each person's best bubble.

The Challenge:

Have one judge with a ruler stand by each contestant. At the signal, contestants have two minutes to blow their largest bubble. Judges will measure each attempt. Have the other teens cheer their teammates on during this contest to keep excitement high. At the end of the two minutes, have each judge announce the largest bubble that he or she measured. The blower of the largest bubble is the winner.

For bubble blowing experts, you may want to have a Double Bubble Contest in which teens blow a bubble inside a bubble. Or have a Loudest Snap, Crackle, or Pop Contest. You'll be amazed at their bubble blowing talents.

CHALK ONE UP

Materials:

Supply each team with a pair of well-chalked erasers.

The Challenge:

Give one contestant from each team a pair of chalk erasers. At the signal, players pound their erasers together to create the largest chalk cloud. Audience response determines the winner.

GIANT SPITWAD CONTEST

Materials:

Each contestant will need the cardboard tube off of a roll of wrapping paper and a few sheets of ordinary notebook paper. Cut the notebook paper into four equal sections. Supply a wastebasket or a bucket as a target for each team.

The Challenge:

Choose two contestants from each team. One contestant will be the catcher holding the basket target at a distance of about ten feet from the shooter. Arm the shooter with paper and the cardboard tube.

At the signal, players roll the paper quarters, stick them in their mouths, and form giant spitwads. After loading their wads in the tubes, shooters blow in the tubes to shoot the wads across the room. The first player to hit the target basket is the winner.

HOME ICK

Materials:

Each team needs one "home ick helmet." These can be made by bolting a colander to a plastic army helmet or by cutting the top out of a cardboard top hat.

Provide each team with eggs, a few baggies of flour, and water balloons.

The Challenge:

This game challenges the teams to get all the ingredients of a cake into their hats. Choose two players from each team and have them stand about eight feet apart. Place the home ick helmet on one player and give the baking ingredients to the other. At the signal, the tossers from each team must land three eggs, one baggie of flour, and two water balloons into their teammates' home ick helmets. The first team to get all the ingredients into the hat is the winner.

PAPER AIRPLANE TOSS

Materials:

This game is a favorite from *Junior High Games Nights*, our first book. Supply enough paper for everyone in the auditorium to have one sheet. You also need several pencils and a small wastebasket as a target. You may want to label the basket "Principal's Office."

The Challenge:

Have everyone in the room write his or her name on a paper and then fold it into a paper airplane. Have all the players line up at the back of the auditorium facing the wastebasket. At the signal, everyone throws his or her plane and tries to land it in the basket. The first one to land an airplane in the basket wins points and six tokens to a video parlor or a coupon for an ice cream sundae.

TONIGHT'S MESSAGE: TURNING YOUR SCHOOL RIGHT SIDE UP

Introduction:

Many teens are here tonight who would like to see changes take place in their junior high schools. Some might like to see better lunches, others want shorter classes, and probably everyone would like to see less homework.

But what about the people in your school? What about the bullies, the druggies, the athletes, and the brains who don't know God? What if they were to change? What would happen then?

Did you know that you can be the one to help make that change? You can be the one to turn your junior high school right side up.

Focus:

Turning your school right side up depends on three relationships.

1. Your relationship with other students (Colossians 4:5-6). One of the most important things you can do to help turn your school right side up is to watch how you act toward other students. You should always show the love of God. You should be different from other students. You should add the testimony of Jesus to a different lifestyle so that others will be drawn to the Father.

2. Your relationship with your teachers (Titus 3:1-2). Our testimonies are no good unless they are consistent with all our relationships. If you tell your friends about Jesus and then talk back to your teachers, your testimony is a lie. You must be careful how you act toward your teachers so as to be a witness to them also.

3. Your relationship with God (Colossians 4:2-3). Nothing is as important as your relationship with God. You cannot turn your school right side up unless you are devoted to God and to prayer. Pray that God opens a door daily for you to share and that he gives you the character to support your testimony. God is a rewarder of those who diligently seek him.

Conclusion:

The only way to turn your school right side up is to have a right relationship with other students, with teachers, and with God. You can start making these relationships right—this instant—by asking God for forgiveness in areas of failure. God can give you a fresh start tonight if you will only ask him.

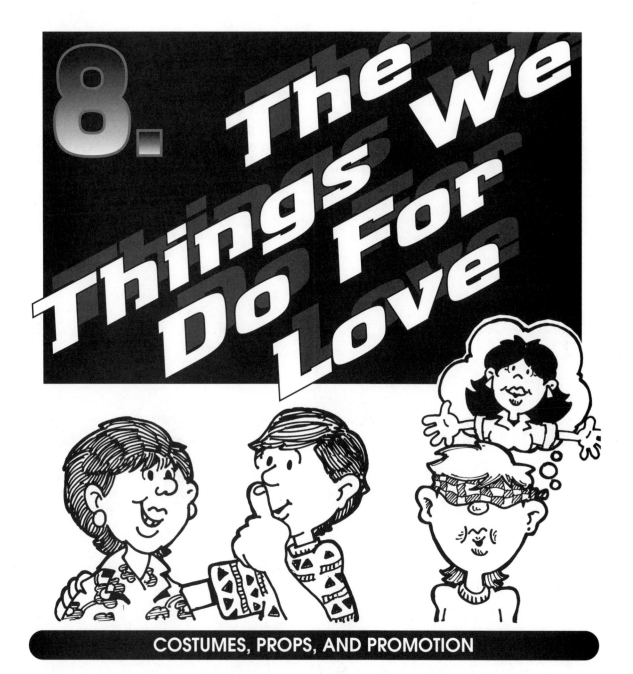

8. The Things We Do For Love

COSTUMES, PROPS, AND PROMOTION

Costumes: Hold the ultimate team spirit night where teens bring in banners and posters showing their love for God and for your games program. Give bonus points to each team that really goes all out with decorations and slogans. This is also a wonderful night for a Great Chocolate Chip Cookie Bake Off, since the way to your host's heart is through his or her stomach. Award a prize or a trophy to the teen with the best home-made cookies.

Props: Cover the stage area with all kinds of store bought or handmade valentines and heart decorations. Place all game props on the stage before the teens enter to heighten interest.

Promotion: The Things We Do for Love

is another great giveaway night. You may want to give away a dinner for two at a local restaurant or a book of McDonald's gift certificates for the ultimate cheap date. Another idea is to hand out one of the great books, tapes, or videos on love, sex, or dating available at your local Christian bookstore.

HEART BREAKERS

Materials:

Purchase four heart-shaped balloons for each team. (If heart-shaped balloons are out of season, use large red balloons.)

The Challenge:

Choose five boys or five girls from the audience for each team. Players line up one behind the other with one of the four balloons between each player. At the signal, the first player turns and hugs the player behind him or her with the balloon in between them. Players squeeze one another until the balloon pops. When the balloon pops, the second player turns to the third and hugs until that balloon pops. Play continues down the line until all the balloons are popped. The first team to pop all the balloons is the winner.

HOPELESS ROMANTIC

Materials:

Each team needs a new rubber boot and a 16-ounce bottle of soft drink.

The Challenge:

Call up one female volunteer from each team who considers herself a hopeless romantic. Ask the girls if they have heard of the man who loved a woman so much that he drank champagne from her slipper. Then bring out the rubber boots full of soft drink. Line up the girls and, at the signal, have them gulp down the soft drink in the boot. The first girl to finish is the winner.

KISSING CONTEST

Materials:

Arrange in advance to have a few of the boys' mothers secretly attend the meeting that night. Provide good, dark blindfolds for your contestants.

The Challenge:

Choose three of the prettiest girls in your group and let them know in advance how the game works. Now choose the boys whose mothers are hiding offstage to be your next contestants. Inform them that you are going to have a kissing contest where they will guess which of these three girls kissed them on the lips.

Blindfold the boys and have them stand with their hands behind their backs, their lips puckered. At the signal, bring the boys' mothers out to kiss them on the lips. Have some of the mothers really plant one on them. After the kiss, watch the guys try to figure out who kissed them. Have them all remove their blindfolds and award points for being good sports. This game is strictly for the laughs, and there will be plenty!

MAIDEN RESCUE

Materials:

Each team needs a roll of thick toilet paper, a folding chair, and a cheap tube of lipstick.

The Challenge:

Choose one girl and two boys from each team. Give the girl the lipstick and have her sit in the chair. At the signal, the first boy, the bad guy, wraps the lovely maiden completely in toilet paper. When he is finished, he runs over to tag off with the other boy, who is the hero. The hero rushes over to unwrap the maiden without ripping the toilet paper. Players should run around the maiden to wrap and unwrap the toilet paper. When the maiden is completely free, she stands on her chair and draws a kiss print on her hero's cheek using the lipstick. The first team to finish is the winner.

MAKEUP MADNESS

Materials:

Each contestant needs a folding chair and a cheap costume wig.

The Challenge:

Everyone spends a lot of time getting ready for a date. This is the perfect chance to show all the boys what the girls have to go through.

Ask some girls who have makeup in their purses to volunteer from the audience. Have the boys sit in the folding chairs. At the signal, the girls have two and a half minutes to get their partners ready for a date. They may use anything in their purses and the wigs you have provided. The team that comes up with the best-looking candidate is the winner.

SWEETS FOR THE SWEET

Materials:

You need one box of chocolates and a book of poetry for each team.

The Challenge:

Choose one boy and one girl volunteer from each team. Seat the girls several feet away from the boys. At the signal, each boy runs up to his partner and hands her the chocolates, dropping to his knees. Each girl rips into her box of chocolates and begins to eat. As their partners eat, the boys must read poetry or sing love songs until all the chocolates are gone. The first team to finish the chocolates is the winner.

TONIGHT'S MESSAGE: THE THINGS HE DID FOR LOVE

Scripture: John 10:15.

Introduction:

People have always been inspired by great acts of love. From Romeo and Juliet, to Anthony and Cleopatra, right up to modern-day romance, we have always been impressed by how far people will go in the name of love.

Focus:

Tonight we want to impress upon you *the greatest act of love ever performed by a man.*

The story is told of a mother and a little boy who lived alone and had a great love for one another. As the boy grew older, he began to notice that his mother had terrible scars on her arms. The boy became embarrassed to be seen with his mother in front of his friends because of the scars. He wondered if he should ask her to cover them with long gloves or a long-sleeved top when they went out. Finally he got his courage up to ask her about the scars.

The mother looked at him with great compassion and said, "When you were a baby, your crib caught on fire. When I smelled the smoke and reached the room, your crib was already in flames. The only way to get you out was to reach through the flames and grab you. The scars show you how much I loved you then and will always love you."

Although this is a tremendous expression of a parent's love for her child, it does not compare with what Christ went through for us.

1. He became a man. Christ left the glories of heaven and intimate fellowship with the Father to become a helpless child on earth, born to a poor, teenage mother. What a tremendous act of love.

2. He served man. Christ came to this earth not to be served, but to serve others. He was always making time for people, loving the unloved, healing the sick, and feeding the hungry. His last expression of love before his death on the cross was to wash his disciples' dirty feet with his own garment. What a tremendous example of true love in action.

3. He gave his life for man. Jesus suffered the most horrible death anyone could suffer when he died on the cross.

Others have experienced tremendous physical suffering, but none can compare to the spiritual suffering of Christ. When he took on himself the sins of every man who has ever lived or ever will live, he experienced the full weight of guilt, sin, and separation from God. Jesus took all of this spiritual suffering upon himself because of his great love for us.

Conclusion:

After picturing the magnitude of God's love, how can you reject the awesome love of the Father? How can you do anything other than surrender your whole life to him tonight? Respond by laying down your life for him. Give him your heart this very night.

9. Chinatown

COSTUMES, PROPS, AND PROMOTION

Costumes: Invite teens to come in their favorite oriental costumes. With the advent of *The Karate Kid* movies and other ninja series, several teens will want to come robed in karate-type clothes. You may even want to hold a Ninja Costume Contest in which teens come in any costume ranging from green ninja turtle shells to head-to-toe black outfits.

Props: Your local party store should carry several decoration items that could assist in decorating your stage area. You may also want to paint a large red sun and some Asian-looking characters on a sheet to be hung as a stage backdrop. Place all game props on the stage before the program to heighten interest as the teens enter.

Promotion: Chinatown is a great opportunity to bring in a missionary from an Asian country. Make sure the missionary knows that this is a youth outreach to your community. You may also want to do a T-shirt giveaway. Cornerstone Creations, 5905 North Kings Highway, Myrtle Beach, SC 29577, sells a T-shirt with John 3:16 written in Chinese that would make a great giveaway.

CHOP FOOEY

Materials:

Supply each contestant with a pair of chopsticks and a bowl of Rice Krispies or a puffed rice cereal.

The Challenge:

Seat contestants at a table with chopsticks and bowls of cereal. At the signal, players begin to eat the cereal using the chopsticks. Something this small is very difficult to eat with chopsticks and the results are hilarious. The first player to finish a bowl of chop fooey is the winner.

EGG ROLL CONTEST

Materials:

Supply each contestant with one hard-boiled egg in the shell and a plastic pig or parrot nose. Using cones or masking tape, mark out a short course on the floor.

The Challenge:

Line up contestants at a starting line. They should be wearing the plastic noses. At the signal, the players must push the eggs through the course using their noses. If a player's egg rolls out of bounds, he or she must pick it up and return to the starting line. Players may bump one another to try to knock another player's egg off course. The first player to roll his or her egg across the line is the winner.

EGG-YOU-FLUNG

Materials:

Supply each contestant with one dozen eggs and a carryout bag or carton from a Chinese restaurant.

The Challenge:

Choose two contestants from each team, one to hold the eggs and the other to hold the carryout bag or carton. Have the partners stand facing each other at a distance of ten to 12 feet. At the signal, players begin to fling eggs to their partners, who must catch them in the carryout bag. The team to take home the most "egg-you-flung" is the winner.

FORTUNE 500

Materials:

Supply each team with a healthy portion of fortune cookies. Make sure you purchase the kind that has repeat or duplicate messages in the cookies. The wrapper should tell you how many messages are inside.

The Challenge:

Seat a contestant from each team at a table facing the audience. In front of each player, place a large basket of fortune cookies. At the signal, players begin to crack open the cookies and eat them. After a player eats a cookie, he or she looks at the message, searching for duplicate messages. The first player to find a matching pair of messages wins.

RICKSHA RACES

Materials:

Construct a ricksha for each team by attaching two six-foot two-by-fours and two lawn mower wheels to the legs of a folding chair. Bracket the two-by-fours to the sides of the chair and place the wheels toward the back by drilling a small hole through the two-by-four through which the wheels may be bolted. When the chair is lifted by the two-by-fours, it will roll on the back wheels. Coolie hats add to the fun and can be purchased from a costume shop or a novelty store.

The Challenge:

Mark out a course that allows the rickshas to make wide turns. Choose two strong contestants from each team. Have one player sit in the ricksha while the other dons the coolie hat and pulls the ricksha. Line up the contestants on the starting line. At the signal, players race to a turning point. At the turning point, the coolie and the rider switch places and turn the ricksha around to race back to the finish line. The first team to cross the finish line is the winner.

SWEET AND SOUR SAUCE

Materials:

Supply each contestant with a lemon, a four-ounce cup of sugar, and an eight-ounce cup of water. Each contestant also needs a jump rope.

The Challenge:

Announce that you are about to make some homemade sweet and sour sauce and that you need a few volunteers. When the volunteers come forward, bring out the supplies. This is your ancient Chinese secret recipe: Take something sweet, throw in something sour, add water, and mix up for lots of fun and laughs.

At the signal, each contestant eats the lemon, downs the sugar, and drinks the water. Then the contestants jump rope 25 times to mix up the sauce. The first one finished is the winner.

TONIGHT'S MESSAGE: THE ONE TRUE GOD

Introduction:

How do we know that our God is the true God? The Asian nations have detailed records of their history and ancestry. They claim that their gods and their religions are true.

Focus:

Tonight we will speak on, *"How can we know for sure that our God is the one true God?"*

1. We can know by his performance (Acts 4:10). Jesus is the one who was crucified and rose from the dead. It is best to get directions to an unknown destination from someone who has already been there. Jesus is the only one who has passed from death to life and has returned to give us detailed directions on how to get to God. Buddha's bones are in the grave, so why should we listen to him? Judge your faith by Christ's performance.

2. We can know by his record (Acts 4:12). His record says that Jesus is the only way to salvation. His record has proven perfectly true for thousands of years, standing the tests of time and adversity. We can trust in a record that has been flawless and unhindered by the plots of man over such a long period of time. That record tells us that Jesus is the only way.

3. We can know by personal experience (Acts 4:13). The men in this Acts account were astonished by the change they saw in the followers of Jesus. I, too, have been astonished by the change in drug addicts, homosexuals, liars, thieves, and egotistical teenagers. God has worked wonderful miracles in their lives that I can see and experience and know to be true, proving that our God is very much alive and active today.

Conclusion:

We may know that our God is the one true God by his performance, by his record, and through personal experience. In performance, Jesus is the only one who claimed to be God who could show reasonable proof. He came to show the way to heaven and ascended there before the witnesses on the hill. Some day he has promised to return and lead his people there. By record, Jesus Christ has a perfect, sinless record. When brought before the most sophisticated legal system of his day, no one could find any fault with him. To this day, Jesus and his word are faultless. By personal experience, the best way to know with certainty that our God is the true God is to experience his forgiveness, his life, and his love for yourself.

With such a mass of evidence and a great crowd of witnesses, how could we ever doubt that our God is the one true God? Why not trust in him tonight? He is the only way.

10. Nerd Night

COSTUMES, PROPS, AND PROMOTION

Costumes: Invite teens to come as nerds, geeks, or their favorite dweebs. Costumes should include out-of-fashion clothes, thick glasses, and other nerdlike features.

Props: Game props should be sufficient to help decorate the stage. You may want to check with a poster store or video rental for some appropriate nerd posters to put up as added decoration.

Promotion: "You don't have to be a nerd to love Nerd Night." "NERD is the Word!" "Free calculator given away!" Any of these could be great promotions for a successful Nerd Night. You may want to preach a message dressed as a nerd. Invite teens to go all out for this crazy occasion.

BOOK BUSTLE

Materials:

Find about 50 old, discardable books. (Check garage sales and old school inventories, or go door-to-door for books.) Hide a gift certificate or a cash prize in a brightly colored envelope in one of the books, and stack the books on a table. Be sure to write down the title of the book in case no one finds the prize. Secure an old-fashioned bell alarm clock or rig a school bell to ring for your signal.

The Challenge:

Choose several nerds from the audience. Inform them that when the signal goes off at any time during the evening, they have 60 seconds to rush to the stage and look for the prize envelope. After 60 seconds, all the players must sit down and wait for the next alarm. The first player to find the envelope wins the prize and the points.

CALCULATIONS

Materials:

Supply a small calculator for each contestant. (These can be collected in advance from your youth group members.) Write five long math problems on poster board using marker pens. Prework the problems and write the answers in pencil on the backs of the problem boards.

The Challenge:

Have contestants sit in folding chairs with their backs to the audience. Announce that this will be a best out of five competition. The first one to come up with the right answer wins each round. Hold up one of the poster boards and shout, "Go!" The first nerd to shout the correct answer is the winner of that round. The nerd to win the best out of five rounds is the grand winner.

LUNCH LAUNCH

Materials:

Supply each team with an empty lunch tray, a spatula, and the following lunch items: one scoop of mashed potatoes, a square of Jell-O, a slimy fish fillet, and a carton of milk.

The Challenge:

Everyone has seen someone trip in the lunchroom and send the lunch tray and food flying across the cafeteria. This game is just the opposite—nerds try to catch their lunch food on their trays.

Position partners about ten feet apart. At the signal, one player uses the spatula to launch lunch items across the room. The other player runs underneath the food to try to catch it on the tray. The team that catches the most food on its tray is the winner.

NERD FOOD

Materials:

Supply each contestant with a bowl of Nerds candy or cereal. If neither of these is available, choose any food that would add to the humor.

The Challenge:

Seat contestants at a table with bowls of nerd food in front of them. At the signal, the nerds begin to eat as fast as they can without using their hands. The first nerd to finish is the winner.

NERD RACES

Materials:

Each contestant needs an oversized pair of pants and a large pair of shoes that lace. The nerdier the clothes the better (check garage sales or thrift shops).

The Challenge:

Choose one contestant from each team. Have contestants slip on the pants and shoes over their clothes. The shoestrings on the large shoes should be tied together. At the signal, the nerds race around their teams while holding up their pants and with their shoestrings tied together. The first player to complete one lap around his or her team is the winner.

T.P. RACES

Materials:

Each contestant needs one large roll of generic toilet paper. Supply a long pencil or a six-inch dowel rod to thread through the toilet paper tube.

The Challenge:

Nerds have the worst luck. Have you ever seen a nerd get toilet paper caught in his or her pants? That is the idea behind this game.

Choose two contestants in costume from each team. Tuck the toilet paper down one contestant's pants at the waist. The partner holds the ends of the pencil or dowel rod so that the toilet paper rolls freely.

At the signal, the nerds run around their teams and around the building in any pattern they want. The only objective is to run until the rolls run out. If the toilet paper breaks, the nerds must return to their rollers to retuck the loose ends into their pants. The results are hilarious to watch. The first team to run out all the toilet paper is the winner.

TONIGHT'S MESSAGE: DARE TO BE DIFFERENT

Introduction:

One of my favorite stories in the Bible is about Zacchaeus. I picture Zacchaeus as this short little nerd who was always trying to fit in. After being teased as a child about his height and lack of athletic ability, he went to school to be successful in business. Now here he is, a rich businessman who has used his position to get back at those who once laughed at him.

But in Luke 19 we see Zac standing on the road to Jericho, still feeling a deep emptiness and sense of need inside. Then the Lord passes by and chooses Zacchaeus out of all those people and goes to his house. What joy must have filled Zacchaeus. Finally someone chose him over the others, someone who really mattered.

Focus:

What happened in Zacchaeus's life to bring about his change in attitude? Tonight we want to speak about *three things that will really satisfy.*

1. He cast off cool (verse 4). When Zacchaeus climbed that tree, he made a decision. He decided that it was more important to have an encounter with Jesus than it was to look cool. Every person must come to this decision in his or her life to be truly satisfied. It is a great relief to any person to quit trying to be cool and just enjoy being saved!

2. He cared for others (verse 8). Zacchaeus decided to quit worrying so much about himself. Instead, he focused on those less fortunate than he was, giving half of all his worldly possessions to the poor. When we feel lonely and unloved, we may find that the greatest joy comes from helping and blessing others. When our focus changes from self to others, we can have true satisfaction.

3. He corrected past wrongs (verse 8). It is one thing to forgive and another to make restitution. We have lost the art today of truly making past wrongs right. Zacchaeus forgave those who hurt him in the past and did everything within his power to correct his own past offenses. Joy comes to those who truly mourn and are sorry for hurting and cheating others.

Conclusion:

The miraculous change that took place in Zacchaeus can take place in any one of us who will follow the same steps of casting off cool, caring for others, and correcting past wrongs and hurts. For every person, these are the steps to true and lasting satisfaction in Christ Jesus.

11. The Christmas Party

COSTUMES, PROPS, AND PROMOTION

Costumes: Invite teens to come as famous Christmas characters. You may want to have a Fattest Santa or Mrs. Claus Contest. Award a prize to the heftiest couple. The Christmas theme gives you several costume options.

Props: Try to get to the store a couple of weeks after Christmas for the great decorations sales. Decorate your back wall with flashing lights, Christmas trees, or even a lawn Santa. Several people will be willing to loan you their decorations out of season.

Promotion: The Christmas Party is great any time of year. After all, it seems that Christmas arrives earlier and earlier every year. Hold a "Beat the Rush; Christmas in September Party!" or a

"Keep the Spirit; Christmas in July Party!" You can also hold The Christmas Party during or near the holiday season, but I think it works even better off-season. Everyone loves Christmas, and there will be a huge supply of props and decorations to borrow in the off-season. You can hold a bizarre gift exchange in which everyone brings a wrapped item that might be used in one of your game nights. Work out a creative gift exchange and get ready to laugh at what kids will come up with. No matter when you hold The Christmas Party, you can be sure that it will be a Christmas to remember.

CHRISTMAS CAROLING

Materials:

Prepare some 30-second cuts of familiar Christmas songs on cassette. We suggest you use familiar songs with humorous artists, such as dogs barking "Jingle Bells," Little Marcy singing "Deck the Halls," or a huge choir singing "The Hallelujah Chorus." And what Christmas would be complete without Bing Crosby's "White Christmas?" What makes these songs funny is the people you choose to sing them. Pass out practice tapes in advance of the game night or have tape players available and send the contestants out for a short practice early in the game night.

The Challenge:

Choose one contestant from each team to do a Lip Sync Contest. Send contestants out to work up routines or have them prepare in advance of your game night. Toward the end of your program, call the contestants onstage to perform their songs for the audience. Choose a winner by crowd response.

GIFT WRAPPING

Materials:

Supply each team with several large sheets or rolls of wrapping paper, tape, scissors, ribbons, and bows.

The Challenge:

From each team, choose one player to be the gift and two others to be the wrappers. At the signal, players use the wrapping materials to gift wrap their teammates. Play Christmas music during the competition. At the end of one song, judge the best wrapping job and award a prize. Then, after the second song, award a prize for the most unusual wrapping job. After the third song, the winner should be the funniest wrapping. Make all the players each take a turn as the gift. Take photographs of all the teams after each round and then make a bulletin board decoration in the shape of a star or a Christmas tree and fill it in with the photographs, placing the overall best gift-wrapped "package" at the top.

HO HO HO'S

Materials:

Provide each contestant with a Santa hat, a cheap costume beard, and a plate of six unwrapped Ho Ho's snack cakes.

The Challenge:

Volunteers are seated in costume behind plates of Ho Ho's. At the signal, Santas eat the cakes without using their hands. The first one finished is the winner.

O, CHRISTMAS TREE

Materials:

Bag an equal amount of tree decorations for each team including garland, tinsel, bulbs, and even lights. You may want to provide tree skirts to be wrapped around the tree "trunks" (players' ankles).

The Challenge:

Challenge each team to make the best-looking human Christmas tree. Let the team choose one boy to be the tree and two or three teammates to decorate. At the signal, players decorate their trees while Christmas music plays in the background. At the end of the song, have judges or the crowd choose a winner. As with "Gift Wrapping," on the previous page, take photographs of the decorated "trees" and make a bulletin board Christmas tree, filled-in with the photos of your kids.

SHOP TILL YOU DROP

Materials:

Pile a table with garage sale clothes. Place a red "sale" tag on one of the garments, and hide it in the pile. If you can arrange for one, put a blue flashing light on a pole with an on-and-off switch. If the light is not available, use any loud signal.

The Challenge:

Choose eight to ten shoppers from the audience. Announce that out of all these garments only one has a sale tag and every shopper is looking for the sale. Whenever the blue light starts flashing (or the signal sounds) at any time during the evening, shoppers have two minutes to rush to the table and find the sale item.

Add some humorous items to your pile, such as giant pants, bloomers, dirty socks, or wild neckties. These items will give an added laugh to the audience. When someone finds the sale item, play stops, points are awarded, and the sale tag is secretly moved to a different item. Run this contest several times during the night. You may want to pick new shoppers each round. The team to find the sale item most often is declared to have the best shoppers and that team wins.

SNOW BLAST

Materials:
Provide a can of whipped cream and a cup of eggnog or cider for each team.

The Challenge:
Bring teams of two onstage one at a time. Have the teammates face each other at a distance of about two feet.

Have one contestant stand perfectly still, balancing the cup of eggnog or cider on his or her head. Arm the other player with the can of whipped cream. At the signal, the player with the whipped cream sprays his or her partner's head, trying to knock the cup off. The first team to knock off the cup is the winner.

TONIGHT'S MESSAGE: THE GREATEST GIFT

Introduction:
We have all probably heard that the greatest gift ever given was God's gift of his Son. Perhaps you have honestly wondered why. What makes that so great?

Focus:
Tonight we are going to speak about *three things that made the gift of Christ the greatest gift ever given.*

1. The gift was given humbly. When God brought Christ into the world, he could have done this in a palace through a princess with international and supernatural fanfare. Instead, God chose for his Son to be born of a teenage virgin in a barn. The event was witnessed only by a few insignificant shepherds. Christ's entire life was a lesson in humility. The best gifts are given privately, individually, and humbly.

2. The gift was given sacrificially. God gave the best that heaven had to offer. He bankrupted heaven to reach down to man. It was with the priceless blood of Jesus Christ that we were purchased. What can a man give in exchange for his soul? What man was unable to do, Christ did in giving his life for ours when he died on the cross.

3. The gift was given unconditionally. God showed us his great love in that while we were yet sinners Christ died for us. He still offers the gift of his Son unconditionally. Knowing that some will mock and reject his gift, he still does not draw back from offering life to those who will choose it.

In Mark 12:41-44, we are told that one day Jesus watched people give their offerings. As you can imagine, many of the rich people threw in large amounts. But Jesus is so unlike the rest of us, he was not impressed with their large gifts. The gift that caught his attention was the offering of a widow whose gift was less than a penny. She gave it humbly without any show or fanfare. She gave it sacrificially; it was everything she had. She gave it unconditionally; with no thought for tomorrow, she gave the gift in faith and love. Her gift was great because it embodied the character of the Father's gift.

Conclusion:

The Father's gift was the greatest gift ever given because it demonstrates the great humility of our God and creator, it demonstrates his fathomless love through sacrifice, and it demonstrates his burden for us through an unconditional offer to receive his dear Son. Have you received the greatest gift yet?

12. Hawaiian Beach Party

COSTUMES, PROPS, AND PROMOTION

Costumes: Invite the teens to attend in appropriate Hawaiian clothes (no swimsuits). Teens can wear flowered shirts or make their own grass skirts to wear over jeans. Hawaiian collectibles, such as pineapples, Hawaiian Punch, or vacation postcards, could be worth bonus points. Others may opt for a Coolest Sunglasses Contest or a Worst Tourist Contest in which teenagers dress as the most embarrassing tourist.

Props: Often travel agencies will have huge cardboard displays of Hawaiian vacations. See if you can borrow one of these for a backdrop. You might have some of your more artistic teens paint a backdrop to hang behind the stage.

Promotion: "Paradise comes to *(your*

game program)." Sounds great, doesn't it? Who wouldn't come? This event works well any time of the year because of the appeal of a Hawaiian atmosphere. Announce the best in Hawaiian entertainment from hulas to luaus to surfing. The Hawaiian Beach Party is fun kids just won't want to miss. Our flyer included a ticket for a free "beach burger" available at our snack shack. Or simply offer a free Hawaiian Punch, Kool-Aid, or soft drink as added promotion.

THE BIG KAHUNA

Materials:

Create a seesaw for each contestant by laying a six- to eight-foot plank across a small sawhorse. Arm each audience member with a water bomb.

The Challenge:

Have each surfer volunteer walk up the plank until he or she is balancing the plank evenly on top of the sawhorse. Surfers should all be holding this position when the starter signal sounds. At the signal, audience members bomb the surfers with their water bombs in an attempt to knock them off balance. The surfer to hold his or her balance the longest is the Big Kahuna winner.

HAWAIIAN LUAU

Materials:

Mix a large amount of "poi" using a super-sized can of vanilla pudding, a large bag of miniature marshmallows, and some liquid Hawaiian Punch. Mix these ingredients in front of your audience, using your hands, with Hawaiian music playing in the background. Slop a few handfuls of the mixture onto a paper plate for each contestant. Provide a plastic pig nose for each contestant.

The Challenge:

Seat contestants at a table as you explain that poi is a favorite food at Hawaiian luaus. Explain that roasted pig is also a luau favorite and, since you couldn't provide this delicacy tonight, you will have each of the contestants wear a plastic pig nose.

At the signal, contestants eat the plates of poi without using their hands. The first player to finish is the winner.

HULA CONTEST

Materials:

Provide each team with a large Hula-Hoop. Mark out a course around your auditorium, leaving room for at least a six-foot track.

The Challenge:

Choose four contestants from each team for a foot race. Team members get inside the Hula-Hoop, holding the hoop about waist high. If there is still plenty of room, squeeze another player into the hoop. Line up all the teams on a starting line. At the signal, players race around the course, crammed inside the Hula-Hoop. The first team to cross the line completely is the Hula Contest winner.

SCUBA-DO RELAY

Materials:

Each team of three members needs a skateboard, a pair of swim fins, a snorkel, and a diver's mask. Attach an extra large balloon to the top end of the snorkel using a double-wrapped rubber band.

The Challenge:

Mark out a course around your auditorium. Line up the contestants as follows: the skateboarder first, the scuba diver (wearing the swim fins) next, and the snorkeler (holding the snorkel and wearing the mask) last. At the signal, the skateboarder skates around the auditorium, returning to the starting line to tag off with the scuba diver. The scuba diver then races around the track in his or her swim fins to tag with the snorkeler. The snorkeler takes one lap around the track and, after crossing the finish line, inflates

the balloon through his or her snorkel until it explodes. The first team to finish wins with a bang!

VOLLEYBALL SPIKING CHAMPIONSHIPS

Materials:

You need three volleyball poles or stands. Use two blankets for a net, attaching them between the three poles using duct tape. On the top of the center pole attach a long spike or skewer. The net should be at a height well over the reach of all contestants. For volleyballs, fill several large balloons with a few ounces of water. Inflate the balloons the rest of the way with air and then shoot a few squirts of shaving cream into the balloons before tying them off.

The Challenge:

Hawaii is a volleyball player's paradise. Divide the group into two teams. Choose four players from each team to line up on opposite sides of the net. At the signal, a balloon is thrown into play.

Players take the balloon and throw it toward the spike. If the balloon hits the spike, a point is scored and everyone is sprayed with the wet mixture. If the balloon misses the spike, it can be picked up by anyone and thrown again. Since the blankets blind the players from seeing the other team, players never know when the shower from a good spike will hit them. This keeps things exciting. After each spike, a new balloon is thrown into play. Three spike points constitute a win.

THE WAVE

Materials:

Supply each person in the audience with a styrofoam cup. At the back of each team, place a full bucket of water. In front of each team, place an empty glass pitcher.

The Challenge:

The idea of this game is to pass a glass of water through the entire team while doing a motion that looks like a wave. At the signal, the last person on each team fills his or her cup with water and stands up with both hands in the air, holding the full cup of water in one hand. As soon as this player stands, the next player stands and his or her cup is filled with water by the first player. The first player then sits down and the water is passed on through the team members as they do "the wave." Have each player let out a shout as he or she stands up. When the wave reaches the front, the remaining water is dumped into the pitcher by the front team member. Another wave is started at the back. The first team to fill its pitcher with water is the winner.

TONIGHT'S MESSAGE: TWO TICKETS TO PARADISE

Scripture: James 2:14-26.

Introduction:

If you were getting ready to board a plane right now to a tropical Hawaiian paradise, you would need two tickets: a boarding pass and a plane ticket. One is no good without the other.

Focus:

Tonight we are going to speak about *two tickets to paradise.*

1. The ticket of faith. We are invited into God's paradise on the basis of faith in the finished work of the Lord Jesus Christ. It is by grace we are saved through faith and not of ourselves. Salvation is the gift of God. He has graciously given everyone a free ticket of faith. Our responsibility is to follow through with that ticket, apply that faith, believe in Jesus, and place our trust fully in him.

2. The ticket of works. Some people think that works have nothing to do with salvation, but Scripture says otherwise.

James argues that if faith alone could save you, then the demons would be saved because they know that God is real. Your ticket of faith must be accompanied by your boarding pass of works. We must show that our faith is valid and true by the accompanying lifestyle of selfless love. One is not much good without the other.

Conclusion:

Do you have two tickets to God's paradise tonight? Some have tried to get there merely by their good works. Others have tried to get to God with a meaningless faith. Let your faith be put into an active expression of the love of God. Let Christ give you two tickets to paradise tonight.

13. Super Special Events: Six Game Night Twists

If one of the game themes in this book just doesn't work for you, try one of these great variations instead.

ALL CHURCH NIGHT

Chances are that by now there are some terrible rumors flying around about what is going on in your game nights. Satisfy people's curiosity by holding an All Church Night in which all the church members can come and watch or come and join in the fun of competition. Include a message at the end with current statistics on teen sex, suicide, and substance abuse. Follow this with statistics on the great response you have seen at the altar. You may want to have a few teens give testimony as to the changes in their lives. This is a great time to make the financial needs of your program known to your congregation.

BEST OF BASH

Gather your favorite games from other nights and put them all into one great Best of Bash! This can be used as a Last Blast Blowout or as a first-night preview foreshadowing some of the awesome game features to come later in the season. Collect your personal favorites from throughout the book and make one incredible night of fun.

FAMILY NIGHT

On Family Night, invite all the teens to bring their moms, dads, brothers, and sisters. Include entire families in your favorite collection of games. When choosing contestants, ask for father-daughter or mother-son combinations. You may want to use mom and dad or brother and sister for some of the great couple games. Invite all the parents to bring their video cameras and to come for the fun. Have a guest or your pastor speak on the value of a Christian family.

FOOD FIGHT NIGHT

Search out every game involving food in this book. Whether it is throwing food or eating food, you are sure to come up with a combination that the teens will never forget.

WATER WARS

Take all the water games from this book and put them all into one wet and wild adventure. Remember to include all the water balloon games, inflatable pool challenges, bucket fun, and drinking contests. Water Wars is sure to be a favorite.

YUCK NIGHT

If your kids are really into the messy games, you may want to celebrate Yuck Night. Select your favorite, most messy games from each of the game nights in this book. Encourage the kids to dress up in their grubbiest grubs or even to wear raincoats and carry umbrellas. Then get ready for the wildest night of fun ever!